Digital Cryptocurrency Bitcoin

Written by
Ralph Manzanares

Table of Contents

Intro to cryptocurrency 5

What are cryptocurrencies? 5

Monetary properties 8

Transactional properties 8

Meet the cryptocurrencies 11

Bitcoin (BTC) 12

Ethereum (ETH) 13

Bitcoin Cash (BCH) 13

Ripple (XRP) 13

Litecoin (LTC) 14

IOTA (MIOTA) 14

Introduction to Bitcoin 16

Bitcoin wallets 21

Asset protection 22

Peer-to-peer system of Bitcoins 25

Banks' interest 27

Safety 27

Liquidity 28

Return 28

Pitfalls of cryptocurrency 30

Bitcoins are widely but not generally accepted 30

No buyer protection.. 30

Fluctuating.. 31

Risk of unknown technical flaws 31

Built in deflation.. 32

Unguaranteed valuation... 32

Why use Bitcoin and other cryptocurrencies? 33

Intro to cryptocurrency

Looking around the world today, cryptocurrencies have become a global phenomenon known to most people, banks, governments, and several companies. Although, it is still somewhat strange and not yet understood by most people.

Beyond the noise, articles, books, and press releases an overwhelming majority of people, even bankers, have a very limited knowledge about cryptocurrencies. They often fail to understand even the basic concepts. This book will hopefully demystify all the aspects of cryptocurrency so that by the time you're done reading you will have a pretty good idea of what cryptocurrencies are, what they're all about, and the investment opportunity embedded in it.

What are cryptocurrencies?

Cryptocurrency is the newest trend in the money market that contains the elements of computer science and mathematical theory. Let's take away all the noise around cryptocurrencies for a moment and reduce it to a simple definition: Cryptocurrencies are a digital, virtual, decentralized currency that uses cryptography for security. Cryptography is the foundation that makes debit cards, computer banking, and e-commerce systems possible. A cryptocurrency is a difficult currency to counterfeit because of this security feature. A defining feature of a cryptocurrency, and arguably its most endearing allure, is its organic nature; it is not issued by any central authority, rendering it theoretically immune to government interference or manipulation.

Cryptocurrencies emerged as a side product of another invention. After many failed attempts to create a digital currency in the nineties, Satoshi Nakamoto, the anonymous inventor of Bitcoin (the first and still most important cryptocurrency), never intended to invent a currency. In late 2008, when Satoshi announced Bitcoin, he said he developed, "A peer-to-peer electronic cash system" with the goal to invent something. Some people even call it the 21st century unicorn, or the future of money. It has been forecast that in the next few years, governments will take large steps towards adopting and instituting a cashless society where people make transactions using decentralized digital currencies.

Basically, cryptocurrencies are entries about tokens in decentralized consensus-databases. Cryptocurrencies are built on cryptography. They are not secured by people or by trust, but by math. It is more likely that a spaceship lands on your house than if a digital currency address was to become compromised.

Cryptocurrencies as an irreversible and pseudo-anonymous means of payment seem like an attack on the control of banks and governments over the monetary transactions of their citizens. They take away the control that central banks take on inflation or deflation by manipulating the monetary supply. No one can hinder someone from using digital currencies, prohibit someone to accept a payment, or to undo a transaction. To better understand the revolutionary concept of cryptocurrencies, let's try to explicitly separate their transactional and monetary properties.

Monetary properties

It's no surprise that most cryptocurrencies limit the supply of their tokens. Their supply decreases and will reach its final number in time. This means that the monetary supply of a cryptocurrency in every given moment in the future can roughly be calculated today. Unlike a government printing more money to pump up the system without backing or by a bank altering a digital ledger (something the Federal Reserve will instruct banks to do to adjust for inflation), digital currencies' supply can't be altered.

Fiat money is created by debt, and the figures you see on your ledger represent nothing but debt. It's simply a system of IOU. Cryptocurrencies don't represent debts, just as gold, cryptocurrencies represent themselves.

Transactional properties

After confirmation, a transaction can't be undone by anybody. Not even your miner nor the originator of cryptocurrency can help you if you mistakenly transfer your funds to a wrong address or if a hacker stole them from your computer.

Neither transactions nor accounts are connected to real-world identities. You receive cryptocurrencies on what are called addresses, which are random chains of around 30 alphanumeric characters.

It doesn't matter if the digital currency transaction occurs between neighbors or someone on the other side of the world. The transactions are propagated nearly instantly following the same process through a network of computers completely indifferent to physical location.

Cryptocurrency funds are locked in a public key cryptography system. The digital currency's address is secured so that only the owner of the private key can send cryptocurrency, making it impossible to break its scheme.

Unlike fiat money and other financial tools, the usage of cryptocurrency does not entail any paperwork or special requests for permission.

Cryptocurrencies are an extremely complicated

arrangement of algorithms simply too difficult to reproduce. They function without the backing of any bank or government. Their intricacy and security from hackers are what gave them monetary value. Cryptocurrency could be the stable force to the nose-diving and destabilized world economy through sales, purchases, and investments, all free from government and banking interference.

Meet the cryptocurrencies

More investors are seeking opportunities to invest their money in profitable ventures like cryptocurrencies. As the demand for cryptocurrency has increased at a rapid rate in the past few years, especially in 2017, it has been a form of encouragement to a lot of investors to invest their money into cryptocurrency rather than investing in penny stocks, mutual funds, or some type of retirement plan. Currently, cryptocurrency is the global trending payment and investment asset. It comes in quite a few forms, all of which are produced by meticulous alpha-numerical computations from a complex coding tool.

There are thousands of cryptocurrencies in the world. Some of these cryptocurrencies are Bitcoin, Ethereum, Ripple, Litecoin, Monero, Dash, Cardano, Waves, and Bitcoin Gold just to mention a few. For the purpose of this book, our focus will be on the Top 10 Cryptocurrencies of 2017. The evaluation is based on the market cap, demand, future scope, and investment value of the listed virtual currencies.

Aside from Bitcoin, every other cryptocurrency is generally called an Altcoin. The prices of each are regulated by the supply of the specific cryptocurrency as well as the demand that the market has for that currency.

Bitcoin (BTC)

Bitcoin still tops the chart as it was the first and most popular cryptocurrency. It is the main reason everyone is talking about cryptocurrency in the first place. This is the origin from which all other cryptocurrencies pattern themselves around. It was invented by Satoshi Nakamoto, who some believe was not actually one person but a group of IT and banking specialists.

Among every other digital currency, it has the highest market cap, with a market capitalization of $301.86 billion and price per coin of nearly $18,020. Currently, there are roughly 16.7 billion Bitcoins in circulation. As it's the costliest virtual currency on the market, it has to maintain its acceptability and legal status in many countries.

Ethereum (ETH)

Ethereum comes second on our Top 10 cryptocurrency list. It is the digital currency that prompted the rise of the initial coin offering. Ethereum is a platform built for smart contracts that is controversial. This cryptocurrency is significantly lower than Bitcoin in terms of current market cap and price per Ethereum token. Ethereum has about an $80.94 billion and an $839 market cap and price per token respectively. At the moment, there are about 96 million Ethereum tokens in circulation.

Bitcoin Cash (BCH)

Bitcoin Cash is a chip off the old block (BTC), which has now matured into a separate cryptocurrency itself. Bitcoin Cash is at the third position on our list with the market cap of $39.91 billion. You can acquire one BCH for $2,366.

Ripple (XRP)

On our Top 10 cryptocurrency list, the much

hyped Ripple stands out as the 4th best cryptocurrency to invest in. Ripple was introduced in 2012 as a real-time gross settlement system network. Unlike the other cryptocurrencies mentioned before, the price is as low as $0.803274 with a market cap of $31.12 billion. Despite its low price, the number of XRP in circulation is as high as 38.74 billion tokens.

Litecoin (LTC)

Number five on our list is Litecoin. It has the market cap of $18.91 billion with a value of around $347.81 for 1 Litecoin. There are a total of 54.38 million LTC tokens in circulation.

IOTA (MIOTA)

IOTA stands for Internet of Things Application. It is a cryptocurrency similar to Bitcoin, but it's different in several key ways.

IOTA does not require the submission of a transaction to verify two other random transactions. This essentially means that it is more decentralized; there's no fee for transactions and the more people using IOTA, the faster the network becomes.

With a market cap of $10,307,582,306 and a market price of $3.71, it comes 6th on our Top 10 list.

Then comes Cardano (ADA), Dash (DASH), NEM (XEM), and Bitcoin Gold (BTG) in the 7th, 8th, 9th, 10th positions respectively.

Introduction to Bitcoin

Despite the fact that companies, investors, governments, and individuals see and handle Bitcoin as real money, some people still aren't familiar with it. Thus, there is this enlightenment about its pros and cons before you make any major decision.

It is obvious that life has been revolutionary since the invention of Internet, making things easier on a global scale. The Internet has made the whole universe a global village. One such online system is the introduction of Bitcoin, a digital currency that can be used for personal and business transactions without an intermediary. All transactions of which can be carried out directly through the Internet. It is sometimes referred to as the currency of the Internet.

This is the first decentralized digital currency, currently with a large market value when compared to other similar currencies. Bitcoin is a form of currency that exists only in the digital world. It turns out to be the new age online payment system that has been active since 2009. The technology behind Bitcoin was created by an individual or a group of IT/banking specialists that has never been identified, but the inventor maintains an anonymous status under the identity "Satoshi Nakamoto."

Unlike other forms of currency, Bitcoin is not printed. Therefore, there are no physical representations of the cryptocurrency; Bitcoin is generated through a process called mining. With the use of dedicated software that solves mathematical problems in exchange for virtual currency, users take control of it by using electronic devices. With the help of numerous platforms such as Blockchain, Coinbase, Bitfinex, Bitstamp, and a host of others, Bitcoin is kept and secured through the creation and activation of virtual wallets.

Similar to every traditional currency, Bitcoin can also perform the same functions like buying investment packages through the Internet. The only difference is that Bitcoin only exists in a digital form.

In contrast to the fiat currency that is being controlled by banks and government policies, Bitcoin gives the user a full sense of belonging such that no government or financial institution has control over it. This is possible because of its decentralized feature. Isn't that an amazing attribute?

Without its user's information being compromised, every Bitcoin transaction is kept in a ledger on the blockchain which is accessible to anyone for research, reference, or review.

Moreover, transactions occur with the use of Bitcoin addresses (a kind of alphanumeric representation) which are not linked to any names, addresses, or any other personal information, making it anonymous compared to other orthodox payment schemes whereby personal information is required.

This is unlike conventional banks that request strings of information, paper documentation, and more personal information. And still, these banks may eventually expose its users to fraud, hacking, or unfavorable policies surrounding the system.

Bitcoin accounts are easy to set up and skip all the unnecessary formalities that banks don't. Furthermore, apart from near-instant processing completion, Bitcoin transactions are relatively small and insignificant without any ability to put a dent in the user's account.

In addition, when you make purchases via fiat currency, you find yourself paying an additional sum of money to the government as tax. Purchases through Bitcoin, however, have no sales taxes that are added. With zero tax rates, Bitcoin can come in handy especially when purchasing luxury items. This is another awesome advantage of using Bitcoin.

Bitcoin mining is limited to just 21 million units, therefore there is almost no tendency of Bitcoin suffering from low inflation as compared to the conventional currencies that constantly suffer from inflation and lose their purchasing strength when governments try to stimulate the economy through quantitative fiscal policies. As predicted by experts, the last Bitcoin will be mined in 2050.

The portability of Bitcoin is another one of its

unique features. A billion dollars worth of Bitcoin can be stored on a microchip and placed in one's pocket.

However, using cryptocurrencies have several disadvantages associated with them. As they are not yet accepted universally, they cannot be used everywhere. More so, their value is volatile because the number of Bitcoins or Altcoins in circulation is quite limited, therefore a slight change in transactions can affect their price. Because of the anonymity of cryptocurrencies, it can be used for criminal acts like fraud. In addition, the irreversible feature could cause the loss of a huge fund if mistakenly sent to a wrong address.

Bitcoin wallets

In order to use Bitcoins, one needs a special piece of software in which you store, send, and receive Bitcoins. This is known as a Bitcoin wallet. This wallet is divided into three types: software wallets, mobile wallets, and web wallets.

Software wallets are installed on computers, mobile wallets are installed on a smartphone or tablet, and web wallets are located on the websites in the form of cloud storage. But all are channeled towards the same goal; allowing users to use Bitcoin for daily transactions. Bitcoin gives them full control over their money.

Making payments using Bitcoins is super easy as it can be done from wallets on your computer or smartphone just by entering the receiver's address, the amount, and then hitting the send button. Smartphones can also obtain a receiver's address by scanning a QR code. Likewise; receiving funds through Bitcoin is just as easy as sending. All you have to do is give the payer your Bitcoin address.

Asset protection

The term "asset protection" refers to the use of a legal strategy in order to hide or shield assets from an economy or a political crisis. And this has been a strategy used by some wealthy and intellectual people from time immemorial.

Considering the recent and unusual economic/political instability across the globe, it is a common thing now to hear everyone ranting about the economy. The Internet and the media are chocked full of news and information about the global economic and political crisis. For this reason, asset protection is gaining so much attention and growing in importance more than ever. This gives rise to the question of how best to protect assets from a sudden and unforeseen economy nosedive.

If you have your assets in banks, I can boldly tell you that they are not safe because your hard-earned money and other assets can be frozen, or even confiscated by the government if anything goes wrong with the economy of your country.

You may also think that storing your assets in the

stock exchange and Forex markets makes it safe. Well, let me burst your bubble by telling you it's not. I have seen great brokers lose investor's money to unfavorable government policies and economic meltdowns.

Are you considering real estate? Well, we are at the peak of real estate investment which could at any moment soon slide downward. When that happens, lots of assets will be lost or have the value drop by half or even more. Furthermore, in times of crisis such as riots or natural disasters, assets in the form of real estate are likely to be a total loss.

Despite the vast array of asset protection methods available, for the purpose of this book, we are going to focus on Bitcoin as a unique way to protect assets.

Due to the fact that it's driven by the free market and not regulated by any government policy, Bitcoins are viewed as a great way to store wealth and make investments or transactions. And it's available for everyone! 'Everyone' means that Bitcoins are open to average people compared to other methods that are made accessible to only the wealthy.

What about the anonymity, security, and portability? Unlike other forms of assets, Bitcoin does not reveal the identity of their owners; it is secured through encryption and passwords known only to the owner, plus add to the fact that billions of dollars can be in your pocket without attracting any attention. Above all, you don't need any intermediaries like an accountant, a broker, or estate agent to handle your assets. You have absolute control over your assets. You can wake up every morning with your assets next to you.

Another aspect of asset protection, which Bitcoin is most effective at, that I would like to draw your attention to is asset protection against divorce suits. In most divorce cases, several people lose a substantial amount of their assets to the other party. But the anonymity and untraceable characteristics of Bitcoin and other Altcoins could save you from losing your assets to greedy divorce lawyers and that greedy spouse who filed just to get your assets.

With the above reasons, one can easily conclude that Bitcoins are the most effective way of securing your assets far from government policy, unnecessary fiscal control from banks, theft, natural disasters, economic meltdowns, political crises, and lawsuits. Yet it is advisable to do it cautiously by having the right protection and risk management procedures in place.

Peer-to-peer system of Bitcoins

Over time, money has evolved from gold to banknotes, to fiat currencies, and now to digital currencies like Bitcoin. In the context of virtual currencies, peer-to-peer (also known as P2P) refers to the exchange of currencies that are not created by a central banking authority. P2P means the exchange or sharing of information, data, or assets between parties without the involvement of a central authority. This approach was adopted in the trading of Bitcoins as a virtual currency. Therefore, there is no central authority issuing new currency or tracking transactions. This is the electronic and collective management of currency transfer by the network.

The peer-to-peer Bitcoin exchange system allows individuals to transfer currencies from one account to another without the hassle of going through any financial institution. Although P2P networks can only operate successfully as digital transfers, it is based on the availability of an Internet connection. Therefore, with availability of a computer or a smartphone and Internet connection, a P2P payment system of Bitcoins grant users the luxury of transacting from the comfort of your home as opposed to going through the pain of visiting banks or other financial institutions.

Banks' interest

Despite all the benefits associated with cryptocurrencies, Bitcoin still faces many challenges in regards to its global acceptability as a medium of exchange (the most important feature that makes any suitable currency). The bone of contention for Bitcoin is whether or not financial institutions will generally accept this virtual currency as a medium for exchange, payment, and collateral. Even critics have pointed to some reasons why Bitcoin may boomerang and why most financial institutions are holding back in accepting Bitcoin. Some of these reasons are: safety, liquidity, and return.

Safety

The absence of a centralized decision making authority makes Bitcoin highly risky. Risks such as a currency split, hacking, identity theft, or outright scams are a recurring problem.

However, measuring the safety of Bitcoin by its volatility, Bitcoin has actually beaten silver, "the world's currency for 400 years."

Liquidity

"Market liquidity as reflected by the amount of trading is still far greater in stocks, fixed income and traditional currencies," Blanch said.

Bitcoin and other rival cryptocurrencies have increased in the recent years, and the trading volume is hard to overlook.

Return

It is so evident that the market capitalization and the value of Bitcoin have more than doubled, and the recent interest in digital currencies has sent their prices soaring. However, cryptocurrency returns will mostly depend on the faith placed in it by individuals, corporations, and financial institutions. It has been noted that the appreciation in Bitcoin prices are due partly to the increasing difficulty of mining Bitcoins, but this could change with the advent of quantum computers or through agreements among developers to adopt simpler protocols.

In spite all this, the banks have been looking into how to incorporate cryptocurrency exchange services into its services for its corporate clients. Banks have been looking into cryptócurrencies for years, trying to create a cryptocurrency-powered wire transfer system.

The proposed system would collect data from external data sources on cryptocurrency exchange rates and use this data to establish its own optimal rate. Although the service is targeted for enterprise-level customers only, this system will allow users to transfer funds by converting the sender's local currency into a cryptocurrency, sending it to a foreign exchange, and then converting it to the destination country's currency

.

Pitfalls of cryptocurrency

Just like every other currency, Bitcoins and Altcoins have their own pitfalls as well. The following are disadvantages associated with using Bitcoin or any other cryptocurrency:

Bitcoins are widely but not generally accepted

Up until now, cryptocurrencies are still only accepted by a few groups of online merchants. This limits the general acceptability of cryptocurrency as a currency.

No buyer protection

When transactions are executed using Bitcoin, or any cryptocurrency, and a party fails in fulfilling his own part of the contract, nothing can be done to reverse the payment. This problem can, however, be solved using a third party escrow service, but then escrow services would assume the role of banks which would cause cryptocurrencies to become similar to a more traditional currency.

Fluctuating

The value of Bitcoins and Altcoins are constantly demand-driven, therefore fluctuating according to demand. This constant fluctuation will cause Bitcoin-accepting sites to continually change prices. It will also cause a lot of confusion if a refund for a product is being made. These are important questions that the Bitcoin community still has no consensus on.

Risk of unknown technical flaws

The Bitcoin system could develop unforeseen flaws. As this system is fully technical and manmade, if Bitcoins were widely adopted and a flaw was found, it could give tremendous wealth to the exploiter at the expense of destroying the Bitcoin economy.

Built in deflation

Since the total number of Bitcoins is capped at 21 million, and the financial worth of each coin will keep increasing as the total number of Bitcoins max out, this system is designed to reward early adopters. Since each Bitcoin will be valued higher with each passing day, it might cause spending surges which will cause the Bitcoin economy to fluctuate rapidly and unpredictably. Hence, deflation.

Unguaranteed valuation

The decentralized nature of Bitcoin is both a curse and a blessing. Based on the fact that there is no central authority governing Bitcoins, its minimum or maximum valuation cannot be fixed or guaranteed. Therefore if a large group of merchants decide to opt out of the Bitcoin system, it will immensely hurt the users who have a large amount of wealth invested in Bitcoin and the system may collapse.

Why use Bitcoin and other cryptocurrencies?

Over the past decade, digital currency has been rapidly gaining public attention, and a good question that everyone must ask themselves is: Should I consider using cryptocurrencies? The answer isn't farfetched. Yes! Everyone should join the train on the journey into the digital world of currency. Bitcoin and Altcoins are just the right steps towards the right direction for global transactions. To neglect the idea of cryptocurrencies on a decentralized network today is comparable to neglecting the idea of the Internet some decades ago. Cryptocurrency is the people's money, and it is also known as the future of currency.

If you have been comprehensively reading this book, you can obviously see that Bitcoin and other cryptocurrencies are gaining global popularity. And without a better understanding of these new digital currencies, how we can transact with them and their effects in terms of global commerce?

Some of the benefits of cryptocurrency everyone should consider when using Bitcoin and Altcoins:

Cryptocurrency is a medium of exchange like normal currencies but designed for the purpose of digital transaction. They promote the ease of sending money to anyone at anytime, anywhere in the world, almost instantly, all without middlemen or excessive fees. Bitcoin and other cryptocurrencies allow everyone, no exception. This includes anyone in the system as long as there is access to the Internet. With a smart device and an Internet connection, you instantly become your own bank and make payments and money transfers.

Cryptocurrencies are fraud proof as all cryptocurrency transactions are stored in a public ledger over the blockchain network. Hence, the encryption of the currency owner's identity that ensures the legitimacy of every record. And because of the decentralization feature, no government or company has control over them.

The technology behind Bitcoin and other cryptocurrencies is accessible to over two billion people who don't have rights to use traditional exchange systems. Compared to other currency and exchange systems, there is no other electronic cash system in which your account is totally owned and controlled by you.

Unlike the conventional financial system that attracts direct or indirect transaction charges, every financial transaction using cryptocurrency usually has no transaction fees. Moreover, all cryptocurrencies are digital and cannot be counterfeited. This also prevents arbitrary reversals of transactions as compared to credit cards or PayPal.

Bitcoin and other cryptocurrencies aren't controlled by any exchange rate, interest rate, or the taxes of any country. It can be used internationally without experiencing any problems.

Because Bitcoin and other cryptocurrencies are digitally encrypted, you cannot be ripped off in a transaction like you can be with conventional payment systems. Compared to a wallet full of cash, it is hard to steal cryptocurrency. There is currently no transaction mechanism that is currently safer and more secure than those that use cryptocurrency.

Opportunities for Bitcoin have gone beyond being just a form of payment. It has grown to providing investment opportunities for investors.

It's more important for prospective Bitcoin investors to pay attention to some facts presented by the advantages and the pitfalls of Bitcoin and other cryptocurrencies. Therefore, for those looking at Bitcoin beyond its functionality as a currency and who wish to utilize its investment opportunity, there are few direct investment options, but it's best that you discuss these with your adviser.

The digital economy, however, shouldn't be understated. As more people are investing their real cash into virtual assets many businesses have begun to accept cryptocurrencies in exchange for goods and services. Even financial agencies are seeing the potential of blockchain technology. Now might be the time to start trading Bitcoin, and to possibly find the coins that have not yet reached their full potential and still have room to rise in value.

Lots of economists and various business experts remain skeptical of Bitcoin. Perhaps the adoption of Bitcoin as a means of daily payment for transactions won't work, but there will be no doubt a cryptocurrency, or a set of cryptocurrencies, that we will be making payments with in the future. Bitcoin and other cryptocurrencies are here to stay, and are indeed the future of money.

Invest now, go crypto.

www.ingramcontent.com/pod-product-compliance
Lightning Source LLC
Chambersburg PA
CBHW071159220526
45468CB00003B/1081